Potty Training Girls
the Easy Way

Also by Caroline Fertleman, MD, and Simone Cave

Potty Training Boys the Easy Way

Potty Training Girls the Easy Way

A Stress-Free Guide to Helping Your Daughter Learn Quickly

**Dr. Caroline Fertleman
and Simone Cave**

Da Capo
LIFE
LONG

A Member of the Perseus Books Group

Copyright © 2011 by Dr. Caroline Fertleman and Simone Cave
First published in the United Kingdom in 2010 by Vermilion, an imprint of Ebury Publishing.

First Da Capo Press edition 2011

Library of Congress Cataloging-in-Publication Data
Fertleman, Caroline.
    Potty training girls the easy way : a stress-free guide to helping your daughter learn quickly / Caroline Fertleman and Simone Cave.—1st Da Capo Press ed.
        p. cm.
    Includes index.
    ISBN 978-0-7382-1454-2 (pbk. : alk. paper) ISBN 978-0-7382-1474-0 (e-book)
    1. Toilet training. I. Cave, Simone. II. Title.

HQ770.5.F473 2011
649'.62—dc22

2010034733

Published by Da Capo Press
A Member of the Perseus Books Group
www.dacapopress.com

Note: The information in this book is true and complete to the best of our knowledge. This book is intended only as an informative guide for those wishing to know more about health issues. In no way is this book intended to replace, countermand, or conflict with the advice given to you by your own physician. The ultimate decision concerning care should be made between you and your doctor. We strongly recommend you follow his or her advice. Information in this book is general and is offered with no guarantees on the part of the authors or Da Capo Press. The authors and publisher disclaim all liability in connection with the use of this book. The names and identifying details of people associated with events described in this book have been changed. Any similarity to actual persons is coincidental.

Da Capo Press books are available at special discounts for bulk purchases in the U.S. by corporations, institutions, and other organizations. For more information, please contact the Special Markets Department at the Perseus Books Group, 2300 Chestnut Street, Suite 200, Philadelphia, PA, 19103, or call (800) 810-4145, ext. 5000, or e-mail special.markets@perseusbooks.com.

10 9 8 7 6 5 4 3 2 1

We dedicate this book to our daughters,
Natalie and Betsy.

CONTENTS

ACKNOWLEDGMENTS

With thanks to Paul Johnson, Judy Cave, and Barbara Levy

Introduction

Little girls are known to be sensible, mature, and generally more advanced than little boys the same age. This is because their brains actually develop earlier than boys'. Boys tend to use just the left-hand side of the brain, which thinks analytically. Girls use both the left-hand side and the creative right-hand side at the same time because the neural pathway between the left and right side is more efficient. This is why girls generally develop language skills earlier, and this difference continues until the age of five, when boys catch up. If this sounds like your daughter, it certainly bodes well for potty training. With a bit of encouragement from you, she should leave her diapers behind with a minimum of fuss and puddles.

Unfortunately, things don't always go by the book. Life can get in the way of the most carefully laid plans. It's well known, for instance, that stressful events such as a new sibling or a move to a new house can have a big impact on potty training. Also, although you hear fewer problems about girls learning to use the potty, all children are different; just because your child is female, it doesn't guarantee she will be mature and sensible. Plenty of little girls are boisterous, slower to mature, and struggle to concentrate.

We've taken all this into account and have written this book to guide you gently through the process of potty training, whatever your situation. Our flexible approach makes the transition from diapers to the toilet smooth, stress free, and fun for all little girls. If you hit a stumbling block, we'll show you step by step how to deal with the problem. By following our potty-training program, your daughter will learn to use the potty in just a couple of weeks—or, if you're particularly lucky, even sooner.

It tends to be Mom who potty trains her daughter, but anyone caring for your little girl can use this book. We've included a special section for dads—it's not always easy for fathers to take their young daughters to the bathroom, so we've given lots of tips.

What Age
Should She Begin?

This is the million-dollar question. In the United States, the average age for little girls is around two and a quarter (two and a half for boys). As all children are different, your daughter may not be ready to potty train until she is older—sometimes nearer her third birthday than her second. She may, however, be ready from as young as eighteen months. There's nothing you can do to change the age at which she develops and becomes ready—this is a function of nature. What you *can* do is observe her carefully and spot the signs that she's ready to begin (see Chapter 1).

Getting the timing right is key to successful potty training. If you push your daughter too early, she'll probably take longer to learn and may even have to go back into diapers for a few weeks. A US study published in the journal *Pediatrics* found that training before the age of twenty-seven months nearly always takes longer than training a child after this age.

Don't be in too much of a rush—it's not a competition. Your daughter won't turn around in twenty years and thank you for the fact that she was out of diapers three months earlier than her best friend. On the other hand, she may well have something to say about the fact that you pushed her into using the potty too soon and she ended up getting stressed and frustrated, still wetting herself at the age of five.

Be patient, wait until your daughter is ready, and the process will be swift with no tears.

Our Method

Our method consists of having potty-training "sessions," beginning with just an hour a day without a diaper and gradually building up until your daughter never wears a diaper at home during the day. The next stage is to leave the house without a diaper (see Chapter 6).

It's a very gentle approach that can be fitted around a busy schedule, even if you work full-time or have other children. You don't have to do a session every day—our method will work if you just manage weekends and perhaps a couple of sessions during the week at bath time. Unlike more intensive methods that take an all-or-nothing approach, there's no need to take a week off work and cancel social engagements while you spend time locked indoors with your daughter, mopping up accidents. Our much more laid-back approach allows potty training to fit around your family and situation.

Bottom, Urethra, or Private Parts?

Choosing a "name" for girls' private parts is never easy. You'll need to think of something by the time your daughter is about one because this is the age she'll probably start playing with herself on the changing table. There's no need to stop her doing this because it's entirely normal—it's natural, inquisitive behavior. She is just exploring in the same way that she may also have discovered and played with her toes, hair, or belly button. It's a good opportunity to begin teaching her the name of her different body parts.

While urethra is the anatomically correct name for the opening from which urine comes, most little girls won't use this term. Another downside of getting too technical is that you could find yourself having to refer to the vagina, labia, and perineum. This would result in a lot of complicated names for a young child to learn, and even if she manages, chances are few other people will understand what she's talking about—particularly her peers.

Try to think of something easy to understand that your daughter will be comfortable saying at school. It's also got to be appropriate to say in front of your pediatrician, as well as other family members. We've found that "private parts" is a good choice.

Other choices that work include "bottom" or "fanny"—again, simple but accurate descriptions. We've also heard all sorts of other nicknames, including "twinkle" and "minkie," which are fine to use if this is what your family is comfortable with. However, do give your daughter an alternative name for when she starts preschool so that she won't risk being teased.

You may also decide to call urine and feces "pee" and "poop"—as we have done in this book. Everyone understands these terms, including teachers, doctors, and children.

1

Is She Ready?

If you try to coax your daughter out of diapers before she's ready, you may run into problems. As we've said before, the average age for little girls to come out of diapers is about two and a quarter, but how do you know if your daughter is going to be one of the early ones or if she needs to wait a bit longer? Well, there are lots of signs to watch out for that indicate she is both physically and mentally ready. If you monitor your daughter closely and get the timing right, you'll find that potty training takes only a couple of weeks with very few accidents.

Although it's known that girls are easier to train than boys, the downside of this is that it puts more pressure on them to come out of diapers earlier. So it's particularly important with girls to ignore competitive friends and family who tell you when they think your daughter should start using the potty. The very best person to decide when the time is right is you.

Even your daughter may be eager to get out of diapers before she's physically ready. However enthusiastic she is about using a potty, if she's not physically developed enough to be able to know when she needs to pee or poop, then she's going to have accidents. This can be particularly upsetting for little girls because most are eager to get things right and to please their parents. You'll have to persuade her to wait a couple of months without dampening her enthusiasm. Explain to her that her bladder ("the bag in her tummy where her pee is stored") isn't yet strong enough but it will be very soon, and when it is, she can try using the potty. If your daughter is reluctant to take no for an answer, then you could also try pull-up diapers. You can call them "big girl diapers" and let your daughter help pull them on.

CHECKLIST:

Signs That She's Physically Ready

☐ *She is able to walk and is stable on her feet.* This is because learning to walk requires intense concentration as your daughter discovers how to use her voluntary muscles. It's too much to expect her to be consistently aware of her bodily functions as well (needing to pee and poop). It would simply overload her system if she had to learn to use the potty at the same time as learning to walk.

☐ *Her bowel muscles are fully developed.* From as young as eight months, your little girl starts pooping at around the same time each day and poops less frequently than when she was a tiny baby. This is because her bowel muscles are developing. By the time she is two, she'll probably be going once or twice a day. But still go ahead with potty training even if your daughter doesn't quite fit this pattern because everybody's different when it comes to bowel movements.

☐ *Her bladder muscles are fully developed.* Bladder muscles mature later than the bowel, usually between twenty months and two years. You'll notice that your daughter has fewer wet diapers until eventually she can go for about three hours or longer without peeing. This is because the urethral sphincter muscles become more developed—these are the muscles that hold urine in the bladder, and as they strengthen, your daughter will develop bladder control.

☐ *She's aware that she's peeing or pooping.* Between the ages of eighteen months and two years, your little girl will develop awareness that she's going to the bathroom. This generally happens a few months earlier with girls than with boys. Your daughter may start telling you that she's peeing or pooping, or perhaps she'll stop playing and squat. She may also tell you when her diaper is wet or soiled.

CHECKLIST:

Checklist: Signs That She's Mentally Ready

☐ *She's happy to try sitting on a potty.* Children need to be mature enough to actually want to use the potty or toilet before you can start training them.

☐ *She's interested in other people going to the bathroom.* Girls tend to show interest several months earlier than boys, which is one of the reasons they tend to come out of diapers sooner.

☐ *She can talk.* As well as being mentally mature enough to begin potty training, your daughter also needs adequate language development so that you can talk to each other about if and when she needs the toilet. And she'll need to understand your instructions and all the praise when she succeeds. As we've already mentioned, language is another area where girls are ahead of boys.

Getting the Timing Right

Timing is important when it comes to potty training. In an ideal world we would all pick a time when we're just following our normal routines because this is when stress levels tend to be lowest. If you've got a big event looming, such as a new baby or a move to a new house, then ideally you should postpone potty training until afterward.

With girls you can sometimes make exceptions. This is because girls tend to find potty training less stressful than boys. Indeed, some little girls learn to use the potty so quickly that it's easy enough to get them trained before big life events. It can be very convenient to get your little girl out of diapers before, say, a new baby arrives.

Wait a Few Months If...

- your daughter has shown reluctance about sitting on a potty or been worried about the toilet flushing. This shows that she is likely to find potty training quite stressful. Coupled with the stress of a big event, it could all be a bit much for her.
- your daughter is anxious about an up-and-coming event—for example, she knows you're moving and seems to be having more tantrums.
- you feel you've got enough to cope with for the moment and having to deal with potty training as well would be just too much stress.

Go for It If . . .

- she can walk, talk (or at least say enough single words to make herself understood), is aware of peeing or pooping, and is enthusiastic about potties. If she's showing all the physical and mental signs we've listed and is eager to give it a try, then she'll probably learn very quickly.
- she's not having many tantrums or acting up. This indicates that she's happy and not anxious about anything.
- she's able to concentrate and doesn't lose patience with what she's doing. For example, she will calmly spend time doing puzzles even if she finds them difficult. This shows that she enjoys learning and so is unlikely to find potty training too frustrating when she has accidents.

If you decide to go for it, be prepared to abandon potty training after a couple of days if it turns out that your daughter isn't ready. This is particularly important if you're attempting to squeeze it in before a big event as stress levels will be higher. So if your daughter doesn't seem to be picking it up quickly, gets confused about when she's about to pee or poop, and doesn't ask for the potty, then you'll have to face the fact that she probably isn't ready.

Don't make too much of stopping potty training. Simply say something like "That was fun, wasn't it? Perhaps we'll try again after the baby is born." Even if she's not yet ready, there's still plenty you can teach her so that when she does finally come out of diapers, the process is as seamless as possible. In the next chapter, we explain how to help your daughter prepare to begin potty training.

Training in Time for Preschool

If your daughter is going to start preschool at the age of three, she'll be expected to be potty trained. Although most little girls are trained long before their third birthday, if your daughter is slower to mature, then you'll feel pressured by this preschool deadline to get her out of diapers.

Try not to pass this pressure onto your daughter because it will delay things further. Call the preschool, explain what stage she is at with toilet training, and they will probably put your mind at rest. They are so used to accidents that they will even have a box of spare clothes.

If they don't sound very understanding, then we advise postponing your daughter's preschool place for a term or even choosing a different, more understanding preschool (it's often possible to get a place at the last minute because other parents may change their plans and pull out). A few months

(continues)

(continued)

won't make any difference in the long run. It's important that she doesn't get upset by unsympathetic teachers if she has lots of accidents. Once the pressure is off, you'll feel a lot more relaxed. Your daughter will pick up on this and will probably learn to use the toilet very quickly.

Do bear in mind that boys tend to have more accidents at preschool than girls, so the teachers won't be expecting your daughter to need constant reminding about going to the bathroom or to have frequent accidents. It's important to mention to them if she needs a bit of help.

It's also common for children to regress in the weeks leading up to the start of the term because they feel a bit anxious about going to preschool. Don't worry too much if your daughter is suddenly having lots of accidents; there's every chance that once she starts preschool, she'll quickly improve.

Our final tip is to take her to the bathroom when you arrive at the preschool, especially if she's not yet accident free. She'll enjoy the child-sized toilets and low sinks and will soon get used to them. If she's at preschool for only a few hours, the chances are she won't need the bathroom again until you pick her up. Don't worry if she does wet herself at preschool (or even soil her pants). Most children have accidents, particularly during their first term, so the staff will be geared up for it.

2

Early Preparation
for Potty Training

From around the age of one, your daughter will start to watch and learn what happens when you go to the bathroom. So even if your little girl isn't yet ready to begin potty training (see Chapter 1), there's plenty you can do to help her in the meantime. Follow our tips, and by the time you take your daughter out of diapers, she'll not only be familiar and comfortable with bodily functions, but also be able to understand how to use the potty or toilet.

Tips for Preparing for Potty Training

Take Her to the Bathroom with You

You probably already take your little girl to the bathroom sometimes because it's more convenient than leaving her outside. Don't stop as your daughter gets older because the more familiar she is with the toilet, the quicker she'll learn to use it herself when the time is right and the less likely she'll be to fear it. You'll find that sometimes she will be more interested in playing with the toilet paper than in watching you, but at other times she'll be fascinated by what you're doing. Don't be embarrassed; she's just curious in the same innocent way that she's curious if you put on mascara or make a phone call. Chat away about what you're doing, and make sure that you wipe from front to back because your daughter will eventually imitate you.

When you wash your hands, encourage your daughter to do the same. This will instill good habits and make the whole process of going to the bathroom into a fun game. You can also let her climb onto the toilet at home (when the seat is down) and flush it. Make this a bit of a treat, saying, "You're such a big girl. Would you like to flush the toilet?" This will increase her confidence and reduce the chances of her becoming frightened of sitting on the toilet or of being sucked away down a flushing toilet.

Public Restrooms

When you're out with your daughter and need to go to the bathroom, the easiest way to take her into a public restroom with you is to choose a wheelchair-accessible toilet and wheel her stroller in. This isn't always an option, however, so you may need to hold her in one arm and go to the bathroom one-handed—not easy but just about possible if you're desperate.

Once your daughter can walk and is too heavy to hold, she'll be busy playing with the lock on the door and the sanitary napkin container while you go to the bathroom. Try not to get upset because it's important that your daughter doesn't associate public restrooms with being yelled at. Instead, you could give your daughter a job such as holding your handbag, and if she still insists on squeezing round the back of the toilet and touching the seat, make sure that you wash her hands thoroughly afterward.

It's important that you wipe the seat of public toilets and sit down rather than squat. Again, your daughter will be watching closely and will imitate you when she's old enough, and she won't be able to squat over a toilet because she'll be too short.

Show Your Daughter Her Dirty Diaper

From time to time show your little girl her dirty diaper and chat about how you're putting on a fresh diaper and cleaning the poop off her bottom. Let her feel the heavy weight of a wet diaper, and explain that it is heavier than a dry diaper because she's peed a lot. This will give your daughter the message that going to the bathroom is a natural process and nothing to be ashamed of. It's important to convey this, so don't ever show feelings of revulsion if you're changing a particularly smelly or leaky diaper.

Don't Get Angry if Your Little Girl Plays with Poop

If you've ever walked into your little girl's bedroom and discovered that she's taken off her diaper and smeared poop over her sheets, herself, and the walls, your natural reaction will have been horror, shock, and revulsion. Surely, little girls just don't do this sort of thing. Well, unfortunately, some do (and boys, too), but it doesn't mean that she's got behavioral problems, and she's certainly not being naughty. She's just being curious. Plenty of children do this— some even taste their poop!

It's important that you remain calm while you clean up, however much you want to yell and scream, because your daughter will be confused if you're angry about her poop. Getting very upset can occasionally lead to your child having "withholding constipation" (see Chapter 9), a condition that can affect toddlers if their caregivers have shown revulsion about their diapers and poops.

If your daughter repeatedly removes her diaper, put her pajamas on back to front so that she can't reach to undo the diaper.

Ensure That Caregivers Are Comfortable Changing Your Daughter's Diaper

Scientists have shown that mothers object to the smell of their own baby's poop less than to that of other people's babies. In a study published in the *Journal of Evolution and Human Behaviour* (July 2006), mothers were given anonymous diapers to smell, and they found the smell of their own baby's diapers "less revolting" than those of other babies.

It's thought that the disgust instinct is overridden in mothers to encourage them to nurture their babies—they would be less likely to do so if they found them repellent. This research demonstrates that caregivers may genuinely find changing your daughter's diapers more disgusting than you do. So be aware of this, and ensure that people caring for your baby don't have any hang-ups that your daughter could pick up on.

Use Bath Time for Practice

Keep a potty in the bathroom from the time your daughter is about fifteen months old so that she can play with it before her bath when she's naked. Tell her what the potty is for and that she can sit on it if she wants to. Your daughter may also like to sit on the potty fully clothed and imitate you when you go to the bathroom, so keep the potty near your toilet.

She's almost certainly too young to actually use her potty, but it's good to have one around so that she's familiar with it. Don't worry if she's not interested. You've got months before you will potty train her, and there's no need to get stressed in the meantime. Let her become curious in her own time, and don't try to force it. If she does happen to sit on it, then do give her lots of praise.

Your daughter is bound to pee in the bath, but you usually won't notice because she'll be sitting. Never try to stop her because it would give negative messages. From twelve months onward she may stand up more in the bath, especially if you use a nonslip bath mat. If you happen to notice her peeing, point it out, saying, "You're peeing! What a clever girl." This will help your daughter to become aware of when she's peeing, and awareness is the first step to control.

Make Use of Her Dolls

Dolls can be useful throughout the toilet-training program. Girls have an advantage over boys in that most of them love dolls. You can buy dolls that pee and have potties, which can be helpful in encouraging your daughter to understand the potty-training process. Any doll can help her learn, however, because you can encourage her to sit it on the potty that you keep in the bathroom. It's a known teaching technique to allow the pupil to teach someone else the skill she is trying to acquire.

• • •

Helping your daughter to be aware of potties, toilets, and bodily functions will give her a big advantage when she starts to actually use the potty. She will already have a pretty good idea about the theory of potty training, and all she'll have to do is put it into practice.

3

Countdown to the Big Day

When your daughter is showing signs that she is both physically and mentally ready to begin potty training and you know that D-day is imminent (see Chapter 1), there are several steps to take. You must prepare your daughter for what's about to happen, prepare your home, and, finally, take your daughter on a shopping spree to buy such items as underpants and stickers. Here's our guide to gearing up for the big day.

Prepare Your Daughter

When you're both feeling relaxed, tell your daughter that you think she's ready to stop wearing diapers quite soon. If you have followed our tips in Chapter 2, she'll have a reasonable understanding of potties and what they are for, and there's a good chance that she will be eager to try using one.

Talk her through the process, and *ask* her if she'd like to give potty training a try. Explain that you'll have to go to the store together to choose potties and underpants. She'll probably be very enthusiastic, but if she's not ready and seems reluctant, that's fine. Tell her that she can wait a few more weeks if she wants to. Some little girls need a bit longer to get their heads around starting something new, and it's much better to let them be ready in their own time than to push.

Once she has agreed to give potty training a try, then tell her when the shopping trip will be and also talk her through what will happen when she has an accident. Explain that she may accidentally pee or poop on the floor or in her new underpants from time to time while she's learning. Emphasize that this is okay because you'll clean it up with wipes and so on, put the soiled underpants in the washing machine, and then give her some nice clean ones to wear. It really helps little girls to understand before the event the process of accidents and cleanup because they can become quite upset if they make a mess or spoil their new underpants.

Prepare Your Home

Choose the room in which you want to begin potty training. If you have a room with old carpets or a floor that's easy to clean, this may be an obvious choice. Make sure the training room is warm enough—you may need to turn up the heating by a couple of degrees during the winter months because your daughter will be seminaked in the early stages of potty training.

You can use plastic-backed bath mats to protect your floor and sofa, with your daughter sitting on the soft side of the mat. If you don't want to risk your carpet getting dirty, you can always set up a play area in the corner of the kitchen if it's big enough. Using the garden is another good option if it's warm enough to play outside. Lots of mothers wait until the summer to get their toddlers out of diapers—as well as sparing carpets, potty training in summer means less washing because children wear fewer clothes in the warmer months. However, there's no need to be limited to the summer because when your daughter is ready to begin, she'll learn to use the potty very quickly and there shouldn't be many accidents.

Go Shopping

Once your little girl has given you the go-ahead that she wants to start using the potty, you can go shopping together for underpants and toilet-training equipment. Talk to her about this shopping trip in advance so that she can look forward to it and have a few days to think about and get used to the idea of getting out of diapers. By the time you hit the stores, she'll be very enthusiastic and will love choosing pretty underpants and fancy star charts.

Shopping List

Here are some useful potty-training gadgets worth buying. Let your daughter make some of the choices, although she obviously doesn't have to be present for every purchase.

Two Identical Cheap Plastic Potties

We strongly advise getting two identical potties because you can keep one in the play area and one in the bathroom and you'll avoid a situation where your daughter refuses point-blank to use, say, the red potty. If you've already got a potty in the bathroom, that's fine because there's no harm in having spare potties that you can keep around your home.

Cheap plastic potties are ideal because they're small and easy to clean. Also, your daughter will squat right down on the floor with her feet on the ground—this is a better position for defecating than sitting on a larger-style potty. Don't worry about potties having splashguards on them; these are to stop boys making too much mess but won't affect your daughter in any way. She can sit with the splashguard at the front or the back, whichever she chooses. Your little girl should definitely be involved in choosing her potty, but you'll have to steer her away from the larger, fancy potties. She'll still enjoy selecting the color.

Underpants

Let her have her say in what she wants. She may opt for something pretty and girly or choose something with her favorite television character. We've found that if she likes her underpants, she'll be eager not only to wear them, but also to keep them dry. If she can't make up her mind, then buy a couple of packs—they'll get plenty of use, especially if you buy underpants in a size bigger than her age (we recommend doing this as it makes it much easier to pull them up and down).

Big Leggings and Tights

Most children don't have the manual dexterity to cope with buttons and complicated clothes until they are about four. So stock up on leggings (not too tight) as these are easy to pull up and down, enabling your daughter to go to the toilet alone when the time comes. Tights in a larger size than she normally wears are also helpful—these will be easier for you to yank down quickly and also easier for your daughter to manage by herself as she progresses. Elasticized pants also work, and jogging-style bottoms are a very practical, albeit unfeminine, option.

Pretty Stickers

Little girls love stickers, so hunt out some that she hasn't had before and thinks are a bit special. A reward chart helps spur on most girls—you can buy a ready-made chart from large supermarkets and office supply stores. Alternatively, make your own using a thick piece of paper or card stock. Write a list of training achievements down one side, such as sitting on the potty, peeing in the potty, pooping in the potty, pulling down underpants, pulling up underpants, and washing hands. You can draw simple pictures for each of these activities and then draw horizontal lines across the chart so that each activity has its own space for stars and stickers. Every time your little girl completes an activity, she gets a star or sticker—you can buy these or just draw on stars.

A Mini–Toilet Seat

Children can find sitting on the toilet quite frightening because it's high up and large enough for them to fall down. So it's important to get your daughter a child's toilet seat that scales down the toilet to her size. We particularly recommend those with side handles as these give your daughter something to hold onto.

A Stepping Stool

This will help your daughter climb onto the toilet, and then she can rest her feet on it for added security. She can also use a stepping stool to reach the sink to wash her hands. You can buy cheap plastic stools designed for this purpose.

A Folding Toilet Seat

This can be helpful when you're out and about because your daughter will feel more secure sitting on a smaller toilet. It will also be more hygienic for her, although you will have to wipe the public toilet seat first so that you don't get your portable seat too dirty. You can buy padded travel seats. Plastic ones are less comfortable but fold smaller.

A Travel Potty

These are particularly useful in the early stages of potty training when your daughter won't have the physical capacity to hold on for more than a minute or two before she pees. The folding potty frame can be whipped out, the legs can be unfolded, and then you can put a bag over the top with a liner at the bottom—or you can put the bag and liner on before you leave home to save time. Once your daughter has been to the toilet, you simply throw the bag away. You can also get portable potties with lids. We don't recommend these, however, as they are bulkier and you probably won't want to carry around your daughter's pee and poop.

•   •   •

Try to begin potty training within a few days of your shopping spree while your little girl is enthusiastic. Help her to put her new underpants away and to put her new potties in place, ready to begin. She can start using her stepping stool to wash her hands right away. Let her play with these new toys if she wants to.

Don't Waste Your Money on These Items

Fancy Potties

Don't fork out money on themed potties, including musical ones or those shaped like animals. If your daughter needs this sort of persuasion to sit on the potty, she's simply not ready to come out of diapers. Also, it's important that her potty isn't so appealing that she won't switch to the regular toilet—we encourage her to start using the toilet within the first couple of weeks of our training program.

Imitation Toilet Potties

Avoid these cumbersome toilet lookalikes, which are large and have lids. They may be more comfortable and appealing to some children, but as we have just said, our program moves from the potty to the real toilet within a couple of weeks, so it's not worth spending lots of money on these big potties. They can also be more difficult to clean than a small plastic potty.

Training Pants

These absorbent cloth pants look and feel like real underpants, but they will make your daughter feel wetter than if she were wearing a diaper. The idea is that your daughter will become more aware of when she is peeing and pooping. We think training pants are a waste of time because when your daughter is truly ready to begin toilet training, she'll know when she's peeing and pooping in her diaper anyway. Training pants tend to be used before children are really ready to come out of diapers. It's harder to clean up soiled training pants than a soiled diaper, which you can simply throw away.

Pull-Ups

Pull-up diapers are marketed as the most grown-up style of diapers for toddlers. We think that they're a bit of a gimmick and tend to be more expensive. That said, we sometimes recommend them for nighttime (when your daughter still needs a diaper at night but feels too grown up to wear one), and also for the occasions when your daughter is insisting on being a big girl and wearing her underpants but you want her to wear a diaper, such as when you're traveling in a car, train, or plane.

• • •

We recommend keeping the potty-training process as simple as possible and just buying what you need to make it a bit more convenient. So although there's a lot of paraphernalia out there, there's no need to get carried away when you shop.

Don't Try to Take Shortcuts

You may have heard of children who skip the potty stage and instead go directly from wearing diapers to using the toilet. Okay, this avoids having to clean poop-filled potties and cuts out a step in the potty-training process, but we think it's better to use a potty. In our program your little girl will move pretty swiftly from a potty to a toilet, but the advantage of getting her on a potty initially is that it puts her in a squatting position, which helps pooping. Also, she will be more likely to sit for longer on a potty, which increases her chances of success. Another advantage is that you won't need to stand over and hold her to help her balance as you would with a toilet.

The only exception we make is if your daughter is big for her age, in which case the potty will be very uncomfortable (see Chapter 5).

4

D-day

So the day has arrived when the diaper comes off and the puddles begin. This can be a bit daunting for both parents and children. This is why our training method has potty-training sessions that last for only about an hour. So there's no need to cancel your social life or take time off work.

It's all very simple. During a session your daughter goes without her diaper at home, and then at the end of the session you put it back on again. The method has been devised to cut the stress of potty training to an absolute minimum. This is important because your little girl shouldn't pick up on any stress and should never feel that by having accidents, she is disappointing you. She will progress a lot more quickly if the process is kept very positive.

Some little girls will learn to use the potty in a few days using our method. By all means, watch your daughter closely, and if she seems able, you can extend the length and number of potty-training sessions quite quickly. However, it's more likely to take a couple of weeks to get the hang of things.

We suggest that you hold back from taking your daughter out without her diaper on for a couple of weeks after she's got the hang of using the potty and toilet at home. It's obviously more challenging to find a public toilet for girls than boys (who can pee down drains or in the gutter). Girls can be particularly sensitive to having accidents and often feel more self-conscious than boys, so rather than put your daughter through any unnecessary stress, wait a little longer before taking her out in public without a diaper.

Plenty of little girls have had success using a more intense potty-training method—the all-or-nothing approach where they stop wearing a diaper and that's it. There's no switching from underpants to diapers, even when you leave the house. You just go for it and hope for the best. Some experts argue that it's confusing for children to keep swapping from pants to diapers, but we haven't found this. After all, children seem to cope with wearing a diaper at night and underpants during the day.

Using our potty-training-sessions approach, you will probably have your daughter out of diapers within a few weeks. Within a few months there's a good chance that you won't even bother to pack spare diapers when you go out.

Before You Begin

Choose a Time

Pick a morning when you and your daughter are feeling happy and relaxed and then suggest, "Shall we try using the potty today?" A good time to ask is when you're changing your daughter's diaper after she wakes in the morning or wakes from a nap. She should be feeling refreshed and happy at these times.

There's a good chance that she'll feel a bit anxious and say no, in which case leave it for a day or so. This isn't a race, and it's important that your little girl doesn't feel pushed into potty training. You can always ask again at bath time when your daughter won't be wearing her diaper.

It doesn't matter what time of day you pick to have a potty-training session, although we suggest that you avoid choosing a time when she's due to poop. If your daughter poops at roughly the same time each day, it can be tempting to time a potty-training session around this. However, there will be too much antici-pation, and she'll sense the pressure. The key to our method is to stay relaxed.

Get Her Ready

When your daughter says yes, and so gives her permission to begin, help her to choose her underpants and to put them on. Try to avoid tights and pants because these will make getting to the potty on time more difficult. Also, your little girl will feel more bundled up, so she will be more likely to forget that she isn't wearing a diaper. You can put on a pair of socks to keep her warm.

Once she's dressed in her underpants, show her where the potty is and put her star chart up. You can also give her a drink—she'll need to pee about twenty minutes after drinking it.

During the Session

Sitting on the Potty

At the start of the session, suggest that your daugh-ter sit on the potty and explain that she has to pull her underpants down. Chances are she won't need to go the first time, but give her lots of praise anyway. Tell her she's a clever girl just for sitting.

Don't make her sit on the potty for too long—thirty seconds is enough, or she'll become uncomfortable and bored. Some training methods suggest sitting a child on the potty in front of a DVD, but we don't recommend this. Our method is about helping the child herself to become aware that she needs to go, rather than randomly catching her pee and poop because she spends so long sitting on the potty.

Wait

Once your daughter has sat on her potty, there's little to do apart from wait and see if she happens to need to pee or poop in the next hour or so. In the meantime, play together and keep an eye out for signs that your little girl needs to pee—she may hold herself or wriggle from side to side. Some little girls will want to hide away if they need to poop or will stop playing and look a bit worried.

If you suspect that she needs to go, then suggest that she sit on the potty again. Try not to ask her to sit on the potty more than once every thirty minutes because she'll find it irritating. After all, she's having one-to-one playtime with Mommy and so won't want this interrupted too often.

Stars

Ensure that your daughter gets at least one sticker per potty-training session—even for putting her underpants on or sitting on her potty. This will help her associate potty training with success. It's important not to make her feel like a failure, even if she doesn't pick it up quickly.

Her First Accident

If her first pee or poop is on the floor, don't allow her to feel like a failure. Say, "Ooh, you've peed and it's made a puddle on the floor because you're not wearing a . . . " and let her fill in the word "diaper." Say, "You're such a big girl that next time you can pee in the potty," and so on.

If she has a pee accident, wipe her, change her underpants into nice fresh ones, and then have her clean up the floor together with you. Be pleasant, but don't give praise, or she'll get confused about where she's supposed to pee.

If she has a poop accident, clean her up with wipes as you would after a dirty diaper. Then dress her in clean underpants, and put her dirty ones in a diaper bag to be dealt with later. Clean up the poop as quickly and with as little fuss as possible. Stay positive throughout—say, "Ooh look, the poop has gone in your underpants because you weren't wearing a diaper, and next time you can poop in the . . . ," and let her fill in the word "potty."

Her First Success

The first time your daughter pees or poops in the potty, go crazy with the praise. Clap, kiss her, phone Daddy to tell him, and award her a particularly pretty sticker. Give her your full attention and loads of praise for at least a few minutes, and she'll soon be on that potty again. The idea is that she gets far more attention for a success than an accident.

Wiping

Explain that when she's wearing underpants she has to wipe herself after using the potty. Then when she does pee or poop, wipe her from front to back "just like Mommy." Don't let her wipe herself just yet because this needs to be done carefully, particularly after a poop, to avoid her getting the bacterial infection vulvovaginitis (see Chapter 9). This is when bacteria are transferred from the anal region to the vagina and vulva.

Let your daughter become used to you wiping her over the next couple of days because she's going to need your help with wiping after a poop until she is about five or six, when she'll be able to competently wipe herself. And you'll need to help her wipe after peeing until she is about three, when she'll have the manual dexterity to wipe herself.

You may need to teach your daughter to wipe herself after a poop when she starts preschool at three—she won't be very competent, but on the few occasions when she's on her own, at least she'll be able to try.

If your daughter is fiercely independent and wants to do it herself, suggest that she tear the paper off the roll so that she feels involved—she'll find this quite difficult.

Over the coming days and weeks as your daughter learns to pee in her potty reliably, she can try wiping after a pee. Show her how to hold the paper and wipe from front to back. A dabbing, rather than a rubbing, action is less likely to result in spreading bacteria.

After the Session

Diaper Back On

As soon as you put your daughter's diaper back on, there's a good chance that she'll pee or poop. This can seem quite irritating as you ask yourself why she couldn't have done this in the potty. However, it's actually a good sign and indicates that she has some control—she was simply feeling too anxious during the session to pee or poop and waited until she was securely back in her diaper again. This will change as your daughter gains confidence over the next few sessions. She will probably pee or poop in the potty within a couple of days because she is obviously aware enough to be able to hang on. All you can do is stay relaxed about where she pees or poops as this will take any pressure off and help her feel in control.

Cleaning Up

If your daughter managed to pee or poop in her potty, then tip the contents down the toilet and wipe the potty with antibacterial wipes. For a more thorough clean, you can also use an antibacterial spray, but do make sure you rinse this off carefully. To clean dirty underpants, use a wipe to scrape the worst of the poop into the toilet, and then rinse the underpants in a bucket before putting them in the washing machine.

Check the Star Chart

Count how many stickers or stars your daughter has earned today. Praise her even if it's just one. Tell her that she can show Daddy when he comes home, and talk about how she can earn even more stars next time—by peeing in the potty perhaps.

Should You Proceed?

After your little girl's first potty-training session, you may feel that she simply isn't ready to come out of diapers yet. The following will help you decide whether to continue (in which case turn to Chapter 5) or whether to postpone potty training for a few weeks. If you decide to postpone it, simply don't mention potty training to your daughter for a little while—there's no need to make a big deal about it.

She Won't Put Her Underpants On

Don't insist that your little girl wear her underpants if she seems to be objecting. This may be her way of telling you that she's not ready to get out of diapers. Before you postpone potty training, try the following:

- Try her with nothing on her bottom half—it may take your daughter a week or so to come round to the idea of wearing underpants.
- Buy some plainer underpants—sometimes little girls are worried about peeing or pooping in their very pretty underpants. Don't worry about wasting money on lots of different underpants—they'll get plenty of use over the coming months.

She Refuses to Sit on Her Potty

Again, this may be your daughter's way of saying she wants to stay in diapers for a bit longer. Before you postpone potty training, try asking if she'd like to sit on a different potty. If her potty in the bathroom is pink with stickers on it, and it's the one she's used to playing with, then she may want to sit on this one rather than the plainer potty you've given her for her potty session. Try swapping the potties, and you may have an instant solution to the problem. (This is why we advised buying two identical potties in Chapter 3.)

She Has Accidents

Of course, children will have accidents during their early potty-training sessions, but you have to work out why. If your daughter was too busy playing to notice that she needed the potty, then continue with the sessions. If, however, she had no idea about when she was about to poop or pee and seemed frustrated or bored during the session, this suggests that she is still too immature to come out of diapers.

Before you postpone potty training, try the following:

- Think back over the last few weeks, and see if you can remember your daughter ever announcing that she needed to pee or poop. This is a good indicator of whether or not she is mature enough for potty training.
- Try having a potty-training session at a different time of day—perhaps when your little girl is less tired or hungry as these factors can make children irritable and unable to concentrate and learn.

In an ideal world, everyone who reads this book will sail through D-day and proceed to the next stage of our potty-training program. We don't expect that to happen, though, and realize that plenty of little girls won't be ready yet. If your daughter is one of these, try to stay relaxed because it really makes no difference in the long run whether she learns to use a potty quickly or slowly.

5
The Next Two Weeks

f D-day went well and your daughter seemed to enjoy her potty-training session, then here's how to progress. Have as many or as few sessions in a day as you like—just do what fits around your schedule and family. Keeping things relaxed in this way will accelerate your daughter's learning. Don't be tempted to cram in too many sessions in an attempt to push your daughter along because this will take the fun out of it. We suggest a maximum of three sessions a day for the first week, gradually extending the time that the diaper stays off. Don't worry if you happen to miss a day or two. It really doesn't matter; you can just carry on where you left off. The beauty of this training program is that it is very flexible.

The following timetable is a rough estimate. All little girls are different, and your daughter may progress faster or slower. It's not a race, and it really doesn't matter whether it takes your daughter two days or two months to get the hang of potty training. The important thing is that it remains fun and that you follow your daughter's lead. So only move onto the next stage when you're sure she's ready, not when you think she should be ready.

Days Two and Three

Continue with the potty-training sessions, reminding your daughter to sit on the potty every thirty minutes or so. Give her lots of praise and stickers. If things seem to be going well and your little girl is enjoying the sessions, feel free to fit in up to three sessions a day, depending on your schedule. You can also lengthen the sessions to a couple of hours or more without a diaper—this will increase the chances of your little girl actually needing to go to the bathroom during a session.

What You Can Expect

The first few sessions will result in accidents and the occasional pee or poop in the potty—usually after you've reminded your daughter to go. You'll notice that she soon becomes more confident about sitting on her potty and pees in it more frequently, perhaps even pooping.

What you're ultimately hoping for is that she will actually tell you that she needs to pee or poop. This is a big milestone because it shows awareness of her bladder or bowel, plus the ability to hold on just about long enough to get to the potty (she'll only be able to hold for a few seconds at first, but this will increase over the next few weeks as she matures). She may ask for the potty only once or twice during the early sessions, but this will increase with time.

How You Can Help

When your daughter asks for the potty, make a tremendous fuss, perhaps rewarding her with a particularly pretty sticker for her chart. If she's slower to ask for the potty and needs lots of reminding, stay calm. Remember that if she's done it once, then she's got the physical capability and her brain is receiving signals that she needs to go, so she is bound to ask for the potty again quite soon.

If she doesn't ask for the potty at all during the first couple of days, don't worry. Just give her longer before moving on to the next stage, and remind yourself that the best way you can help is by allowing her to progress at her own pace. In the meantime continue to give her lots of encouragement, with a sticker every time she sits on the potty, pees or poops in it, or washes her hands.

Days Four to Seven— Using the Toilet

Once your little girl has hit the big milestone of being able to ask for the potty, you can show her how to sit on the toilet. Note that she still won't be asking for her potty every time she needs to pee or poop, so do keep reminding her (although you won't be reminding her as often now).

What You Can Expect

Most little girls are willing to try sitting on the toilet but may take a couple of days longer to actually pee or poop in it. Eventually, your little girl should be as confident about peeing and pooping in the toilet as she is in her potty. Soon she'll hardly bother with her potty.

How You Can Help

Suggest that your daughter try sitting on the toilet at bath time (she won't be wearing clothes, and you'll both be near the toilet, so no last-minute dashes). If she refuses to sit on the toilet, then respect her decision and simply repeat the suggestion in a couple of days. As long as you stay relaxed, she'll soon try.

Give your daughter masses of praise for simply sitting on the toilet, even if she doesn't go—the toilet can seem very big to small children, and the flushing can be a bit scary. When she does finally pee or poop in the toilet, give plenty of praise and stickers.

Continue to allow your daughter to pee in the potty if she wants to because she will have come to associate it with getting lots of praise. Be prepared, too, for her to have days when she doesn't feel up to the challenge of using the toilet. Never give your daughter the message that there's anything wrong with using the potty. In fact, travel potties can be invaluable when you're out and about and there are no nearby restrooms (see Chapter 3).

Week Two—More Practice at Home

Continue doing the sessions and having your daughter use the toilet at home until she rarely wears a diaper during the day and is able to tell you more than 50 percent of the time that she needs the toilet. Children still need a bit of reminding for weeks, and sometimes months, after they're potty trained. The aim is to build your daughter's confidence before you venture out so that you can minimize accidents outside the home.

Garden Practice

If you've got a garden, then encourage your little girl to squat down and pee in it because this will be an immense help when you're out. Because small children have small bladders, they can't hang on long, so if you're not near a restroom, you may have to take emergency measures. If your daughter is comfortable with peeing behind a tree, this will sometimes save her having an accident. So teach her to pee in the great outdoors—a skill she will occasionally resort to right into adulthood!

What You Can Expect

Your daughter will soon become more or less toilet trained at home. She may even take herself to the toilet, although this usually takes a few weeks longer. You can expect her to have the occasional accident for a couple of months. Don't worry—just react as normal in a calm, reassuring way.

How You Can Help

It's essential that you remain relaxed and avoid putting pressure on your daughter. Just give her lots of encouragement, and watch her confidence grow.

Troubleshooting

She Willingly Sits on the Potty but Seems Unable to Pee

Lots of little girls sit on the potty but don't seem able to pee. This is because they aren't yet physically mature enough to know when they need to pee. If this is the case, you need to give your daughter another month or so to mature, so stop the potty sessions for now. Don't make a big deal about stopping the sessions because you don't want your little girl to feel like a failure.

If your daughter is particularly big or tall for her age, she may feel hunched up and uncomfortable on the potty. You could try moving straight to the toilet, but do use a child's toilet seat so that she feels secure.

She Becomes Tearful Every Time She Has an Accident

Some girls hate spoiling their pretty underpants. Explain to her how easy it is to clean her underpants—she can help put the underpants in the washing machine and switch it on. Perhaps she could try not wearing any underpants for a few days while she builds confidence in peeing and pooping in her potty. It's important to give masses of reassurance about accidents and to tell your daughter that even Mommy and Daddy (and any other adults she admires) had accidents when they were little.

She Refuses to Sit on the Toilet

Little girls tend to be quite brave compared with boys, so your daughter will probably be willing to sit on the toilet. If she is hesitant, then help to build her confidence by allowing her to flush away the pee and poop from her potty. Once you've tipped it down the toilet, reward her by letting her climb onto the closed seat so that she can flush the toilet as a special treat. Without realizing, she'll come to associate getting on the toilet as a treat rather than something scary.

It's important not to pressure her into sitting on the toilet. This has to be done in her own time— all you can do is casually suggest she give it a try. Ensure that you've got a child's toilet seat installed plus a stepping stool, as both of these help children cope with the large size of a toilet.

She Won't Put Her Diaper on to Go Out

If your daughter is reluctant to wear a diaper when you're going out, by all means allow her to go diaperless if you think she'll probably be okay (see Chapter 6 for more on coping when you're out and about). Children sometimes know their own capabilities better than their parents. However, if you're pretty sure it will end in tears because she's not ready, persuade your daughter to wear a pull-up diaper—grown-up travel pants. Pull-ups are also useful for long car journeys, and your daughter can always change into her underpants on arrival. Alternatively, you could use a travel changing mat to protect her car seat—tell your daughter it's a travel mat to make her more comfortable.

If she's adamant that she wants to wear her underpants and refuses even to wear a pull-up, let her have her way. There's nothing to be gained by letting this become a battle. Be especially kind if she has an accident and resist saying, "I told you so," however tempting, as you struggle to clean her up in public.

By the end of this stage of the program, your daughter will no longer wear a diaper at home and will be comfortable about using the potty and toilet. If she needs more time, that's fine. All children are different, and it's important that she's happy about leaving her diaper off before you move on to the next stage, which is going out without a diaper on.

6

Out and About

After a couple of weeks you can think about taking your daughter out without her diaper on. Although potty training girls is usually easier than boys, when it comes to going out, it can be a bit more challenging because they can't easily pee against the nearest tree or down a drain. It's therefore important to be sure that your daughter is physically capable of hanging on before she pees. You can do this by not rushing to the bathroom when you are at home—take your time, and see if she is able to wait.

Another tip is to try teaching your daughter to sit on your toilet at home without her child's toilet seat. This can be very useful for using public toilets. Some children (especially those who are tall or agile) will be happy to do this. Whenever your daughter sits on an adult-sized toilet seat, do hold her firmly so that she feels secure and doesn't worry about slipping down the toilet.

If your little girl seems apprehensive about the big seat, don't push it—just buy a fold-up children's toilet seat (see Chapter 3). These fit easily onto public toilet seats to make them smaller and easier for your daughter to sit on. Let your daughter practice

CHECKLIST:

Checklist: The Going-Out Checklist

☐ She doesn't wear a diaper at home during the day.

☐ She usually tells you when she needs to pee or poop.

☐ She can hang on a couple of minutes before peeing or pooping.

☐ She is confident about sitting on a toilet (or a fold-up toilet seat).

☐ She's happy to use a travel potty.

Once you've ticked all of these items, you can take your daughter out and be reasonably confident that she will remain dry. There are bound to be some accidents over the next few weeks, so pack spare underpants and tights, wipes, and a plastic bag to put soiled clothes into. We also suggest protecting the stroller with a travel changing mat for the first week or so—mainly to minimize your stress and keep things nice and relaxed.

with it at home so that it's familiar. It's also worth investing in a travel potty (see Chapter 3). Again, let your daughter have a go at using this before venturing out. There's a chance that you'll never have to use it, but it will give peace of mind during those early trips out.

Your First Trips Out

Your first outing could be to the supermarket, a local café, or a (tolerant) friend's house. Don't go too far from home in the first week—a day trip in the car is obviously more likely to result in accidents.

Tell your daughter where the bathroom is when you arrive and ask if she needs to go. Chances are that she won't even go to the bathroom on her first few trips out, especially if you keep them short. This stage is about confidence building, so when you get home, do tell your daughter how clever she is to have gone out without her diaper.

It's worth reminding little girls to go to the bathroom whenever you happen to be near one. This will reduce the number of tedious public restroom searches. Get into the habit of asking if your daughter needs to pee before you leave home and whenever you arrive somewhere with a bathroom. She may be wary of using an unknown toilet, so tell her you need to go and suggest she come along, too. It's worth finding out where the restroom is in your local supermarket, library, or anywhere else you may visit in the early weeks because when your daughter needs to pee, you won't have long to get her there.

Public Toilets

Take wipes to wipe the seat and some tissues in case there's no toilet paper. Also pack antibacterial hand gel in case there's no soap to wash hands afterward. Some public toilets are particularly dirty, which can be tricky for little girls because they aren't tall enough to squat over the seat. Wipe the seat before lifting her onto it, and then hold her securely. Your daughter is bound to touch the seat and perhaps the floor when she bends over to be wiped. Try not to express any disgust as this will make her feel anxious; just use lots of wipes and antibacterial hand gel.

You can buy disposable paper toilet-seat covers. We don't recommend them, though, because they slip and your daughter may not feel secure sitting on them. It's also important that she doesn't grow up being too fastidious about public toilets—we all need to use them, and there's no point being too uptight about them.

Contrary to popular belief, you can't actually catch anything from toilet seats. The only real risk is if your daughter touches the seat, gets some infected poop on her hands, and transfers the germs via her mouth, which could give her a stomach bug and diarrhea. This can be avoided with good hand washing.

Nowhere Near a Bathroom

There will be times when your daughter announces she needs to pee or poop and there's just no way that you can get her to a bathroom in time. You have a few options.

1. Squat

You may be able to find a quiet spot, perhaps behind a parked car, where you can help her squat. If you're in the country or a park, then she might be able to squat behind a tree. She will probably get pee on her underpants and tights, but don't worry too much—urine is sterile and will soon dry off. Some mothers hold their daughters over drains as this is less messy, but it's also back-breaking and not recommended.

2. Use the Travel Potty

This is a good option if you've got it with you, especially if your daughter needs to poop.

3. Put a Diaper On

It's worth keeping an emergency diaper in your handbag in the early days because you can put this on your daughter whenever she needs to pee or poop. This is a good solution when you're on public transport with no toilets because a portable potty could spill. Explain that it's just an emergency diaper and that she can take it off again as soon as you are able to clean her up.

Public Accidents

Some little girls are quite self-conscious about wetting themselves and will be even more distraught if they soil their underpants. Make sure, therefore, that you are organized with a cleanup kit (wipes, diaper bag, clean underpants and tights) so that you can clean up your daughter quickly and efficiently, minimizing her embarrassment.

Ideally, take her into a baby change area or a wheelchair-accessible toilet where you can stuff her soiled clothes into a plastic bag, clean her up with wipes, and give her clean underpants and tights (or trousers). If there's nowhere available, not even a public restroom nearby, then find a quiet corner and change her out of wet clothes as quickly as possible to avoid fuss and embarrassment. Don't worry about wiping away pee because being a bit damp after peeing once won't do her any harm.

If she's soiled her underpants, it can be trickier to clean her up, but again try to find a quiet corner and peel off dirty clothes carefully, sealing them in a plastic bag. Use wipes to clean up the worst of the poop—there's no need to do a perfect job in an emergency because you can do a thorough cleanup at home. Just change her into clean clothes.

Never get cross with your daughter for having accidents because she'll find this upsetting. She may even recognize it as a new device to get Mom's attention, in which case you can expect more public accidents in the future. Keep your manner low-key but pleasant: "Oops, you've pooped in your underpants.

Next time we can find a grown-up toilet, and you can get a special star."

Dads—Taking Your Daughter to the Men's Restroom

When out, dads are often very embarrassed about taking their daughters to the restroom, but there may be emergency situations when they simply have to. The first hurdle is finding a toilet. A wheelchair-accessible toilet is generally the best option. If there isn't one available, you'll have to take her to the men's restroom, in which case carry her straight into the cubicle to avoid her becoming curious and wandering off. Don't worry about the other men at the urinals—some will be dads and full of admiration, others will feel pity, and the majority won't even notice you.

Once inside the cubicle, give the seat a wipe with an antibacterial wipe (use toilet paper if you don't have wipes with you). Be quick because your little girl won't be able to hang on for long. Help your daughter onto the toilet (the wheelchair-accessible toilets are usually quite high up). Use a portable toilet seat if you have one, and offer to help hold your little girl on the toilet—she'll know what she wants.

When it comes to wiping, your daughter will probably be able to wipe herself after peeing, so just make sure she has a couple of sheets of toilet paper. Don't worry too much if she doesn't do a particularly good job—it's only pee. If she does poop, it's a different story as your daughter may still struggle with this. You'll need to wipe her from front to back to avoid infection. Make sure that you both wash your hands thoroughly afterward.

The Next Few Weeks

Once your daughter has become used to leaving home without her diaper, she's as good as potty trained. She'll become used to using public restrooms when necessary and to pee before leaving home. As she matures, she'll also find that she can hang on for longer.

There will be occasional accidents—it's very common for three-year-olds to continue to have accidents every now and again—but you'll find that your daughter gradually becomes confident about taking herself to the bathroom unannounced at home, only asking for help with wiping after pooping. Accidents will become such a rarity that you'll soon start leaving the travel potty and eventually the change of clothes at home.

Encourage your little girl to use the toilet without her child's toilet seat because this will make going out much easier—you can always reintroduce the star chart as an extra incentive.

7

When Your Daughter Doesn't Fit the Mold

I t's all very well giving a week-by-week guide to potty training your daughter, but little girls are all different and some simply won't comply. If this applies to your daughter, the following extra strategies will enable you to customize our potty-training method so that it works for her.

The Rebel

G irls are naturally quite savvy, and some will work out that accidents equal attention. Plenty of little girls have resorted to pooping and peeing for attention. This is particularly common when a new sibling arrives, leaving your daughter feeling very put out. It can also occur if there are other family stresses and your little girl isn't getting as much attention as she's used to.

Although it's shocking and disgusting to see your little princess deliberately pooping in her underpants like an angry convict, try to understand that she's still a baby herself and desperate for Mommy's love and attention. Your daughter is especially likely to protest while you're breastfeeding the new baby because your attention will be instantly diverted from the baby to her—even if it is angry attention. As far as she's concerned, attention is attention and it makes no difference if it's angry attention.

Be reassured by the fact that protest pooping is normal and doesn't mean your daughter is deeply disturbed. It's easily dealt with by minimizing your response. This is easier said than done, but do resist the temptation to freak out and yell because this will pretty much guarantee that your little girl repeats her performance. Pop your baby in his crib, and clean your daughter up quickly and calmly without being chatty, using plenty of wipes and shoving dirty clothes in a bag to be dealt with later. Only start chatting and giving attention again to your little girl once you are settled back and feeding the baby.

Bear in mind that you were probably cooing over your newborn adoringly while your daughter watched unnoticed. Try giving your daughter a special dose of mommy attention while you are breastfeeding by singing, telling stories, or even watching children's television together. You could also try talking to her about her feelings—ask if she finds it difficult seeing you cuddling the baby because she wants a cuddle herself. Explain that babies take up a lot of time, but once the baby is asleep, then you can have a lovely cuddle together. If she doesn't want to talk, just leave it. Your little girl will probably try protest pooping a few more times. Keep spare clothes and wipes at hand so that you can clean up really efficiently. If you keep your reaction consistent, she'll soon give up.

Protest pooping can sometimes occur when parents are particularly nice about cleaning up accidents. By all means give yourself a pat on the back for remaining calm when there's poop smeared around your home, but be careful that you don't inadvertently give your daughter a huge dose of kindly attention. We're not suggesting that you should get annoyed, but try to keep your response more neutral—aim to be calm and efficient rather than calm and kindly. When the mess is cleaned up, don't say much about it, but switch to doing something completely different, and only then give your little girl lots of chatty attention.

The Enthusiast

Some little girls are desperate to come out of diapers and wear pretty underpants like their older sister, cousins, or friends. Although they are mentally ready, they are still very young and probably don't yet have the physical capabilities. The best way to deal with this is to give potty training a try to avoid this becoming a battle. Explain to your daughter that she can go without her diaper for a morning to see how she does. Do give her lots of praise for sitting on the potty, pulling her underpants up and down, and so on, even if she proves incapable of knowing when she's about to pee or poop. After her session, give her lots of praise and tell her that she can have another go at using the potty another day—hopefully she'll forget about it for a little while before wanting to try again.

In the meantime you could let her have her own underwear drawer so that the concept of growing up will still seem within her grasp. She'll probably enjoy taking her underpants out and admiring them, perhaps trying them on dolls.

The Artist

If your daughter loves painting and coloring, you may find that she becomes so absorbed in her drawings and has such excellent concentration that she sometimes wets herself. Becoming very involved in play is probably one of the most common reasons for girls to have accidents.

The problem will naturally resolve itself as the signals to go to the bathroom become stronger with age, and also as her bladder develops, allowing her to hold on for long enough to finish her picture. In the meantime you can suggest that your daughter go to the bathroom before her coloring, and don't make too much fuss when she has an accident. Just explain that she was concentrating so hard that her body didn't notice that it needed to pee—keep positive so that your little girl doesn't become self-conscious and worried about having accidents.

The Child Who Doesn't Mind Wet Underpants

Most little girls are fastidious about hygiene and won't stand for being in wet underpants. As a result, they will tell you the moment they have wet themselves and be eager to change into clean clothes. Because they don't like being wet, they will be motivated to learn to use the potty quickly. Not all little girls are like this, however, and some really won't care about being wet.

If your daughter is quite laid back and happy to play for hours wearing wet underpants (a characteristic more often seen in little boys), do check her underpants and tights regularly to see if she's had an accident. She may end up a bit sore if she's wet for a long time. When you do discover that she's wet but hasn't told you, don't make a big deal about it. Just say, "Oh, you've peed. Let's get you into nice fresh clothes."

Don't give her extra attention—positive or negative. Remind yourself that she's not deliberately peeing in her pants; she's still very young and simply learning. Okay, it may take her a little longer to learn than if she were more aware of being wet and soggy, but she'll get there before long, and the day will come when she's dry all the time. In the meantime you can console yourself with the fact that she's not a fusspot.

The Contortionist

Little girls with older brothers may insist on peeing standing up. If they push their stomachs out, it's just about possible for girls to pee into the toilet while standing or against a tree, although it will probably be a bit messy. Watching your daughter standing to pee will seem a bit strange, but she isn't weird, and it doesn't mean she'll grow up to be butch—she's just copying her brothers, so don't make a big deal about it. You'll probably find that she grows out of it as soon as she starts preschool and sees other little girls peeing (at preschool, the toilet doors are usually very short and don't lock, and lots of children happily go to the toilet in full view of each other).

The False-Alarm Child

You've just got to the front of the line at the bank and your little girl announces, "Mommy, I need to poop." Your obvious reply is "Can you wait a couple of minutes?" To which her obvious response is

"No, it's coming now." So you lose your place in line, curse as you realize you'll have to come back to the bank another time, then race off to find the nearest restroom. When you get there, your daughter sits down and then calmly explains that she doesn't need to go anymore.

Many parents would lose their temper at this point, but that really isn't the answer. False alarms are quite common when children are toilet training, and your daughter may get genuinely confused from time to time about whether she needs to go to the bathroom or not. Also, the stress of rushing to find a restroom can sometimes stop her needing to go. If you react, this can easily become a great new device for getting your attention; or worse, it could make your daughter feel anxious about asking for the restroom next time. So bite your tongue, resist getting annoyed, and simply say, "Oh well. You can always try again later." False alarms may go on for a few weeks and can be very tedious. Resist showing you're annoyed in any way, and the problem will resolve itself.

The Late Starter

Although lots of little girls have the physical ability to control their urine and bowel movements soon after their second birthday or earlier, there are plenty of exceptions. Don't push your daughter if she's a late starter because the pressure will make her feel anxious, especially when she clearly lacks the physical capability to progress. If you push her too soon, she'll probably fail, and you'll have to restart potty training in a few months, dragging out the whole process.

Girls who are late starters are quite unusual as it tends to be boys who are the slow ones to come out of diapers. You're bound to know other little girls of her age or younger who are already potty trained. You have to do what is right for your daughter, though, and in this case it is to be patient and proceed with potty training only when she's showing the signs of being physically ready (see Chapter 1). There's also a chance that she's late to become mentally ready—again, unusual for girls, but it happens. You must wait before proceeding until she is showing the signs that she has the mental maturity (see Chapter 1).

If your daughter is one of the slower ones to come out of diapers, it's important to abandon any preconceived ideas you may have had about getting her potty trained by a certain age. Instead, remind yourself that she will get there in the end. If she's six months behind her friends or cousins, so what? If you don't care, she certainly won't. In the meantime, you'll probably get a few comments and helpful suggestions from well-meaning friends and relatives. Don't give in to their pressure. Be confident that you are doing what is right for your little girl—after all, you know her best. Explain to helpful friends that your daughter isn't yet showing the signs that she's ready to come out of diapers, and when she is ready, you'll perhaps try out some of their suggestions. Grandmothers can be trickier because they are from a generation that tried to get children out of diapers as early as possible, driven by the fact that they may have used cloth diapers and possibly didn't have a washing machine. Reassure them that you are intending to start potty training your daughter within the next few months or so, but you are watching for signs that she has the physical capability. If all else fails and they keep going on, you could show them this book!

If your daughter ever starts asking why other girls wear underpants rather than diapers, simply use this as a cue to give potty training a try. If it turns out that she still isn't physically ready, see the section "The Enthusiast" earlier in this chapter for tips on persuading her to wait.

How to Resume Potty Training After a Failed Attempt

If your daughter has reached the age of three and is showing no willingness to use the potty, it's probably because you tried to train her before she was mature enough or at a difficult time, such as the arrival of a new baby, and she's come to associate potties with stress. She won't be the only one. You, too, will dread getting the potty out because you know it ends in accidents and tears.

You can resolve this. Although your daughter is old enough to be physically ready to come out of diapers, you need to help her to become mentally ready too because at the moment there's a bit of a block. Put her back in diapers for six weeks, and don't mention potties or underpants unless your daughter does first.

After six weeks, ask your little girl if she'd like to try again using the potty. She will probably say no because she's testing you and making sure that the pressure really is off. So let her have her way and say, "Okay, maybe another day." Resist mentioning

(continues)

(continued)

potties for another week, and then ask her again. Don't appear anxious or in any way bothered that she's not interested, and she'll probably agree after a couple more weeks. You can give her extra encouragement by showing her a package of chocolate candies and saying that she can earn these as well as stickers for every time she sits or pees on the potty. Although some parenting experts would frown on giving children sweets as bribes, plenty of mothers will testify that it works. Once again, let your daughter be the one to decide whether today is the day.

When she finally agrees, she has effectively given her permission to restart potty training and so will be feeling in control and a lot less anxious than before. You will probably find that she learns very quickly. It's very unlikely that she won't ever agree because she'll be aware of other little girls her age using the potty or toilet and will eventually want to be like her peers.

8

Night Training

The first time your daughter goes to bed without wearing her diaper, you'll no doubt be bracing yourself to be woken in the small hours to change bedding and nightclothes. Although bed-wetting happens to pretty much all children from time to time, the upside is that girls generally have fewer problems with wetting the bed than boys and tend to remain dry through the night earlier.

Girls often manage to stay dry at night around the time of their third birthday, a few months after they have been potty trained. Do remember, though, that all children are different and develop at varying rates. Some little girls will find it physically impossible to stay dry through the night until they are four or five. One in six five-year-olds regularly wets the bed. However, bed-wetting is rarely anything to worry about (see Chapter 9 to rule out any underlying medical problems). You can take comfort from the fact that health professionals don't even recognize bed-wetting as a problem until the age of six because it is so common among small children. You need to seek help from your doctor only if, after the age of six, your daughter is wetting the bed more than twice a week.

As a parent, it's important to take a relaxed approach and to reassure your daughter so that she doesn't become anxious about wetting the bed or having to wear a diaper at night. It's particularly difficult for girls who are late nighttime developers because they will be different from most other girls their age. Try not to worry that there's anything wrong with your daughter or even that it is your fault in some way. You just have to accept that there's nothing you can do to speed things along because it's all a matter of your daughter's physical development, and this is controlled entirely by nature, not nurture.

How the Body Develops to Stay Dry at Night

It's impossible for your little girl to have night control until she is physically mature enough. This is what must happen:

- She needs to produce enough vasopressin. This antidiuretic hormone suppresses urination at night by slowing the production of urine. It tends to kick in at around eighteen months, although in some children it doesn't do so until the age of six.
- Her nervous system must be mature enough. This will enable it to trigger a strong signal during sleep telling her that her bladder is full and needs emptying. This signal needs to be strong enough to wake her and so must be stronger than the full-bladder signals she receives during the day. This is why children usually learn to be toilet trained during the day before they can go without diapers at night.
- Her bladder needs to be large enough. This will mean it can hold a large enough quantity of urine to avoid needing to get up throughout

the night. Bladders grow rapidly from the age of two until four, explaining why lots of children come out of night diapers once they are three.

When to Leave the Night Diaper Off

Most little girls will be ready to go without their night diaper a few months after they manage to be dry during the day—often around their third birthday and usually before the age of four. Girls generally find night control easier than boys, and some will learn to stay dry during the night at the same time as they come out of daytime diapers. Try leaving the nighttime diaper off while potty training if you think your daughter is physically ready. More than three wet beds in a week suggest that she's not yet physically mature enough and should go back to night diapers.

Early Signs That She May Be Ready to Try

- She remains dry during her nap. This is one of the first indicators that your daughter has some control over her bladder during sleep. Once she is potty trained, put a fresh diaper on for her nap and see if it's still dry when she wakes up. You can start leaving her diaper off once she has had ten consecutive dry naps.

- She is able to hold on for a pee. This shows good bladder control. As your daughter matures, you'll notice that she is able to hang on longer before she pees. Once she can wait several minutes, you could try leaving her diaper off at night if she's keen to give it a try.

- She says she doesn't want to wear a diaper at night. Lots of little girls are desperate to be grown up and will decide themselves when they are ready to abandon their night diaper. You may well find that she is indeed ready to stay dry at night, but some girls overestimate their maturity and will end up wetting the bed. Give it a couple of weeks, and use diaper mats and towels to save on laundry. If, however, she's having more than three accidents a week, you could gently suggest that she wait a few more weeks for her body to be ready. If she's reluctant, then try getting her into pull-ups.

Definite Signs That She Is Ready to Try

- She wakes up during the night to pee in the toilet or potty. This shows she is well and truly ready to leave her night diapers behind. Her brain's signals that she needs to pee are now so strong that they wake her up. Be aware that most children don't get up to pee during the night if they are wearing a diaper.

- Her diapers are still dry in the morning. This is a sure sign that she no longer needs to wear a diaper at night. She now has enough of the hormone vasopressin, which suppresses night-time urination. If she has had several consecutive dry morning diapers, let her have a diaper-free night. Note that some children will pee in their diaper as soon as they wake up and won't use the toilet until they are not wearing a diaper.

When your daughter shows at least one of these signs and has only very occasional accidents during the day, you can try leaving her diaper off at night.

How to Come Out of Night Diapers

Get Her Permission

Ask if she'd like to try leaving off her night diaper, and go ahead only if she seems eager. If there is any reluctance on her part, simply postpone the big night for a couple of weeks or until your daughter is happy about the idea. It's important that she doesn't feel pushed into leaving off her diaper because she'll get particularly anxious should she have an accident. Also, feeling stressed can sometimes make children more likely to wet the bed.

Buy a Big Bed and a Night-Light

It's essential that your little girl is out of her crib and in a big bed before she starts night training, or she won't be able to get to a potty or toilet during the night. You can leave a potty by the bed (not ideal if the bedroom is carpeted) or leave the potty in the bathroom nearest her bedroom. Some little girls will happily use the toilet during the night, especially if they have become used to using the toilet, rather than the potty, during the day.

Make sure that there is either a night-light in your daughter's bedroom or a hall light on so that your daughter can easily find her way to the toilet or potty during the night. If she does get up in the night to pee, encourage her back to bed quickly. Don't give too much praise in the middle of the night, or she'll become fully awake and may even want to play.

Protect the Bed

Use a mattress cover under the sheet—the plastic ones get a bit sweaty, so we suggest you use a cotton-quilted one (available from most stores that sell bedding). You can give extra protection by putting a disposable diaper mat or a towel under your daughter's bottom in the early weeks. These can be whipped out in the middle of the night, usually leaving the bed dry underneath.

Monitor Her Drinking Pattern

Ensure that your little girl has plenty to drink during the day because dehydration can irritate the bladder, making her want to pee more frequently.

Once you're sure that she's getting plenty to drink, you can stop giving her drinks in the hour before bedtime. It may take a few days to adjust your daughter's drinking pattern.

Remind Her to Pee Before Bedtime

Get into the habit of reminding your daughter to pee before she goes to bed. If she's been in bed a while before lights out, ask if she needs to pee before going to sleep. Offer to help her get out of bed because she may be feeling too tired to bother otherwise.

Wake Her for a Night Pee

Your daughter may sleep up to twelve hours at night, which is a long time for anyone to go without peeing. It may be worth getting her up to pee during the first couple of months of night training to reduce her chances of wetting the bed. Make sure that you wake her up and that she doesn't pee in her sleep, which will lead to bad habits and make bed-wetting more likely.

When you wake her, usually before you go to bed yourself, you may find that she takes ages to actually pee and sometimes doesn't seem to need to go. Once you've helped her onto the potty or toilet, ask if she needs to pee—she may be able only to nod or shake her head as she'll be too tired to speak. Also, try turning on a tap as the sound of running water may help her to pee. You'll find that after a few nights she gets used to being woken up to pee and will be able to perform a bit quicker. There will be occasions when she simply doesn't need to go, so do accept this and pop her back to bed. There's still a reasonable chance she'll stay dry until morning.

What to Do When She Wets the Bed

It's not a matter of *if* she wets the bed but *when*. Just about all children will wet the bed when they are learning to remain dry through the night. This means having to wake up and change bed linen. Stay calm and never show any signs of irritation with your daughter. Keep spare nightclothes and sheets at hand so that you can get your daughter settled quickly. If you've put a towel or diaper mat down, you may find that the sheet is still dry underneath, which makes things very easy.

The Next Morning

Make a big fuss over your daughter if she managed to remain dry. If she did wet the bed, don't worry or get upset—it wasn't your daughter's fault and shows that she's not physically mature enough to stay dry every night. Never assume it was because she was too lazy to get out of bed to pee. Be patient, and kindly explain to your little girl that our bodies grow up at different rates and that hers is still changing so that one day she will find it easy not to wet the bed.

Should You Continue?

When your little girl starts night training, do bear in mind that a few accidents are completely normal and to be expected. However, if she's having more than three accidents in a week, then her body probably isn't yet mature enough, so put her back in diapers for a month or two. If she's staying dry most nights and having only one or two accidents a week, persevere because in a couple more weeks she'll have even fewer wet nights. Should she get very upset by the accidents, you can always pop her back in night diapers to allow her time to mature a little more.

Troubleshooting

She Refuses to Wear a Diaper at Night

L ots of little girls are eager to be "big girls" and will make a fuss about wearing a diaper at night even if they keep wetting the bed. Try persuading your daughter that pull-ups are big girl night diapers, or let her decorate a pull-up diaper with felt-tip pens and stickers during the day and call it "princess night underpants." Tell her she's allowed to wear it only at night, and come bedtime she will hopefully be eager to put it on.

It Seems Impossible for Her to Learn to Stay Dry at Night

Plenty of little girls still need night diapers when they are four and may wet the bed occasionally even when they are five. Some will remain in night diapers until they are six. If your daughter is a late developer, it's essential never to pressure her; accept that her body simply isn't mature enough for her to stay dry at night. Just give her masses of reassurance, and talk to her about bladder size and brain signals. Explain that once her body is ready, she will find it easy to stay dry every night.

She's Been Invited to a Sleepover but She Still Wets the Bed

Being a late developer is particularly hard for girls as they are more socially mature than boys and many start to have sleepovers from about the age of four or five. Sadly, there's no magic way to make her stay dry at night when she stays with friends, and she'll actually be more likely to wet the bed if she's anxious.

When she gets the sleepover invite, do ask her if she actually wants to go—she may decide that she doesn't because of the risk of wetting the bed. If she does want to go, then mention her bed-wetting to the other child's mother, and tell your daughter that she can tell the other mother if she does wet the bed.

We suggest buying night pants, which are pull-up diapers in pretty designs shaped to look more like underpants than a diaper. They are disposable, and your daughter could wear one under her pajamas. You can also buy incontinence briefs online. These don't look as diaperlike as the disposables and are basically briefs with a sewn-in absorbent pad. They are available in tiny sizes, from two to three years and upward.

Just like potty training, night training can't be rushed. When it happens will be very much dictated by your daughter's physical development, and all you can do in the meantime is gently guide her and be very patient.

9

Resolving Common
Medical Problems

When children have trouble with potty training or bed-wetting, you just have to wait patiently for them to mature and the problem will usually resolve itself. Occasionally, however, there is a medical condition at the root of your child's training troubles. If this is the case, then you'll need to see your doctor. Here are some conditions to be aware of.

Urinary Tract Infection (UTI)

This is ten times more common among girls than boys because girls have a much shorter urethra (tube that leads from the bladder to outside the body), which makes it easier for bacteria to enter the body. If your daughter suddenly starts to wet herself after being dry for a while, or she wets the bed more often, it may be due to an infection. This is because urinary tract infections cause more frequent peeing. Other symptoms to look out for include peeing only a small amount at a time, pain on urination, fishy-smelling urine, a fever, vomiting, and abdominal pain.

What You Can Do

Although anxiety can be the reason for bedwetting or more frequent accidents, you should take your little girl to the doctor in case she has an infection. A simple urine test will show if there is an infection that needs to be treated with antibiotics. To help prevent reinfection, and to help stop your daughter getting a urinary tract infection in the first place, always wipe her from front to back. This reduces the chances of bacteria from the anus entering the vagina. Also, give her plenty to drink because a faster and more frequent flow of urine gives bacteria less time to multiply in the bladder.

Vulvovaginitis

Lots of little girls suffer from this when they come out of diapers. Gut bacteria (found in poop) are transferred from the anal region to the vagina and vulva, causing inflammation, soreness, and itchiness. It's therefore important that little girls have help wiping thoroughly and from front to back.

Although baby girls can get covered in poop, they generally don't get vulvovaginitis because their diapers are changed quickly. Once out of diapers, though, if a little girl does a bad job of wiping herself after pooping, she could remain a bit dirty for hours on end until she has a bath or someone checks and wipes her properly—perhaps when she gets home from preschool or school. Also, once little girls are out of diapers, they can scratch themselves, making the skin around the vagina and vulva more vulnerable to infection—and of course touching themselves can transfer infection.

Vulvovaginitis isn't serious and doesn't affect girls after the age of about eight as the body prepares for puberty and starts to make estrogen, which strengthens the vaginal skin.

What You Can Do

Your doctor may take a swab and prescribe antibiotics, antibacterial cream, or estrogen cream to help minimize any discomfort. You can take steps to try to avoid the condition in the first place and to manage it if your daughter does suffer because it can be quite uncomfortable. Whenever possible, then, help your daughter to wipe herself—especially after she poops—and always from front to back. If she's fiercely independent, let her have the first couple of wipes and then say something like, "You've done so well I bet Mommy can't wipe anymore off." Cotton underpants and avoidance of bubble baths can also help reduce irritation, and do keep your daughter's nails short to minimize scratching the skin.

Thrush

This is a fungal infection caused by *Candida albicans*, which thrives in warm damp conditions such as the vagina. As well as being sore and itchy, thrush has a thick white discharge. Thrush isn't a sexually transmitted disease—it's a common infection that can affect people of all ages. It's often seen

after antibiotics for another condition such as ton-
sillitis or an ear infection.

What You Can Do

If you suspect your daughter may have thrush, seek
medical help because this fungal infection is easily
treated. Your doctor will probably prescribe an anti-
fungal cream, and you should see an improvement
within a couple of days. It's important to continue
the treatment after symptoms have disappeared to
prevent a recurrence. Again, cotton underpants can
help because the cooler your daughter is, the less
prone she will be to infection.

Diabetes

Every year, according to the Centers for Disease
Control, more than 13,000 young people in
the United States develop diabetes mellitus—the
amount of sugar in the blood is too high, and the
excess glucose is passed out of the body in the urine.
If your daughter has diabetes, she will pee a lot more
and be very thirsty, even getting up in the night for

a drink. She may also seem generally lethargic and unwell, and sometimes children with diabetes will suddenly start having more accidents and wetting the bed.

What You Can Do

Get medical help because diabetes must be managed with insulin injections. You will also be told how to help balance your daughter's blood sugar levels by ensuring that she eats regularly and sticks to particular foods.

Constipation

Dry, hard poops and straining on the toilet are sure signs of constipation. Address this quickly because constipation can become painful and your daughter may start to withhold her poops and make the problem worse. It may even cause anal fissures (discussed in the next section).

If you don't take care of this condition, your daughter could develop chronic constipation and overflow incontinence. This is when dry, hard stools become lodged in the back passage and any poop that manages to get past gets squashed, broken up, and looks like diarrhea. You may notice that her underpants are smeared with poop even if you're sure that her bottom is being wiped properly. Eventually, your daughter will start soiling her pants because the poop that is lodged in the rectum confuses the sensations in the bowel and she won't know when her bowel is full and she needs a poop. The final stage of chronic constipation is that she will become unable to tell when she needs to pee and start wetting herself.

What You Can Do

- See your doctor, who will confirm constipation by feeling your daughter's stomach and rule out any rare anatomical problems. Sometimes an X-ray is arranged to confirm this. Your doctor may prescribe laxatives and stool softeners.
- Stress can make constipation worse, so reassure your daughter that it's not her fault if she's been pooping in her underwear.

- Make sure that your daughter drinks plenty because dehydration can slow bowel movements.
- Gradually introduce more fiber into her diet by giving her more fruit, vegetables, dried fruit, beans, cereal, and whole wheat bread. It's important to increase her fiber intake very gradually because a sudden, large increase will probably cause gas, bloating, stomachache, and diarrhea.
- If your daughter's poops have been dry, hard, and painful, she may have become anxious about going to the bathroom. Make sure, though, that she doesn't hold on when she needs to go because poops can change from soft to hard in a few hours. Get her to the toilet quickly when she says she needs to poop, and encourage her to go by reassuring her that pooping won't be so painful if she goes now rather than later, and if she drinks plenty of water and eats the fibrous food you give her. Explaining to your daughter what constipation is and how you are taking care of it will help her to feel less anxious.

Anal Fissure

A small tear in the anus can cause very painful pooping and also some bleeding (the bleeding is nothing to worry about once a fissure has been diagnosed). The cause of fissures is usually constipation— forcing out hard stools. Your daughter will be reluctant to poop, particularly in the potty or toilet if she's only recently started potty training. If she's in pain, she'll opt instead for the familiarity of her diaper.

Straining can also cause anal fissures. A bit of pushing is fine, but if your daughter is really struggling, then suggest that she tries to poop a bit later instead (usually another five minutes or so). Straining can be a sign that she's a bit constipated, so do watch her diet and fluid intake.

What You Can Do

S ee your pediatrician because it's important to get a diagnosis, particularly if you spot any bleeding. Your doctor may prescribe a soothing cream to put on your daughter's perianal region (the area around the anus). Healing can take a while because the skin in the anus is wet. A small dab of Vaseline to lubricate the anus just before your daughter poops can help alleviate discomfort.

Because anal fissures nearly always result from constipation, it's essential to take care of this. Do follow all the tips on avoiding constipation as this condition can make anal fissures particularly painful. The fissure won't be able to heal if your daughter remains constipated.

Attention Deficit/Hyperactivity Disorder, Autism, and Other Learning Difficulties

Learning difficulties make potty training particularly challenging, and if your daughter is affected, you'll need masses of patience. Don't attempt to get her out of diapers too soon because having a false start would be very disruptive for her. You want to be sure that she is physically ready.

What You Can Do

Follow our method. This should work well as it aims to minimize the pressure put on the child. Be prepared for potty training to take longer than it takes other children. Ask your doctor or whoever helps you with your daughter's condition about getting some help with potty training. They may also give you some advice and tips that are relevant to teaching your daughter.

Frustrating Days

If your daughter's toilet training is delayed because of a medical condition, then be reassured that there is plenty of help available. On those frustrating days when you think she'll never succeed, just remind yourself that she will get there in the end—and what's a few extra months anyway?

10
Moving Forward

When accidents are a rare occurrence and your daughter is confident about going to the bathroom, we say that she is potty trained. Although this happens relatively painlessly for most little girls, some will take a while to reach this stage. If your daughter is one of the slower ones, it will sometimes feel as though she'll never be reliably dry, but she will get there—probably without you even noticing. You'll suddenly realize one day that your daughter hasn't wet herself for a while.

Whether your daughter was quick or slow to come out of diapers, over the coming weeks and months you'll see her becoming more independent—taking herself to the bathroom without even asking and needing less and less help with wiping and hand washing. Her new skills will give her lots of confidence, and you and your daughter will feel proud as she makes this momentous step away from her baby years toward becoming a little girl. When she goes on play dates and starts preschool or school, she'll be at a big advantage and will feel more confident about being away from you because she is fully toilet trained.

Accidents and Setbacks

Diarrhea

Diarrhea is common among toddlers, and if your daughter picks up an infection, she is likely to soil her diapers. This doesn't mean that she's regressed; she's simply unwell. We suggest that you put her back in diapers for a day or so to save on mess. Be sensitive to your daughter, and explain that a diaper will just be worn while she's ill and needs to rush to the bathroom. Tell her it's difficult to get to the bathroom in time, even for adults. If she's very reluctant to wear a diaper, then don't force her—she's unlikely to have diarrhea for more than about twenty-four hours.

Wetting the Bed

If your daughter is dry during the day but still wets the bed or even needs diapers at night, she is still, by our definition, potty trained. Staying dry at night relies on your daughter being physically mature enough, which is all a function of nature, so we always say that nights don't count.

Dealing with Accidents

Once your daughter has been dry for a while, don't worry if she suddenly has an accident. Most children wet themselves between the ages of three and four and sometimes will even poop in their pants. Although common, it generally happens only a couple of times a month, so your daughter is still potty trained. Once again, it's simply a waiting game for parents as your daughter matures and slowly stops having any accidents at all.

When she does have an accident, she may feel as though she has failed because she will have come to associate using the toilet with lots of praise. Make light of it so that her confidence isn't diminished. Tell her that even big girls have accidents sometimes, and perhaps say, "Never mind, these things happen.

You must have been too busy concentrating on your coloring to remember to go to the bathroom."

Dealing with Setbacks

Sometimes your little girl will have more than just a random accident and will start wetting herself frequently, despite having been dry for months. Setbacks generally occur when she is stressed and can happen around the time of starting preschool, the arrival of a new sibling, or perhaps moving to a new house. Your daughter may start wetting herself in the run-up to these stressful events or once they have occurred. The best way to deal with a setback is not to deal with it. Make light of any accidents. Remember that accidents can also be a way of getting attention, which is another reason not to make too much fuss.

Some little girls will want to start using their potty again or even to wear a diaper. If this happens with your daughter, let her. She's only trying to be the much-loved baby, so give her plenty of fuss and attention. She'll soon get fed up with soggy diapers and messy potties. Setbacks don't generally go on for more than a few weeks, so keep your response to your little girl's regression low-key and wait for it to pass.

• • •

We hope that you and your daughter have enjoyed our relaxed approach to potty training. We would like to leave you with some checkpoints to assess your daughter's progress.

Ten Signs That Your Daughter Is Fully Potty Trained

1. You no longer even think about packing spare underpants and tights for her when you go out.

2. If she doesn't pee before she leaves home, it's not a problem—you won't be searching for a bathroom within the next ten minutes.

3. Her pretty underpants are starting to look old and worn out.

4. The potty has become dusty and forgotten because she uses the toilet.

5. If you're going away for the night, you pack only one nightdress for her and don't bother taking a spare.

6. When you visit your local café, you no longer glance over at the restroom to check there isn't an out of order sign or a long line.

(continues)

(continued)

7. When you go somewhere new, you don't do an automatic check to see where the restrooms are the minute you arrive.

8. She knows how to wipe from front to back and can wash her hands by herself.

9. You don't have to plan bathroom stops on long car journeys—she goes when everyone else goes, and there's never a wet car seat.

10. At home, your daughter trots off to the bathroom by herself without even telling you.

Checking off three or more of these points shows that your daughter is well and truly toilet trained, so well done. If you can't check off these points, then your daughter isn't there yet, so keep up the encouragement and praise and be patient. It will happen, we promise. In a couple of months or so, diapers and potties will start to become a distant memory, and when you hear other mothers earnestly discussing the perils of toilet training, you'll wonder what on earth all the fuss is about.

INDEX

ABOUT THE AUTHORS

Dr. Caroline Fertleman is consultant pediatrician at the Whittington Hospital, London, and is honorary senior lecturer at the Royal Free Hospital and University College London Medical School. She is also honorary consultant pediatrician at the world-renowned Great Ormond Street Hospital for Children. She lives in London with her husband and three children.

Simone Cave was the health editor at the *Daily Mirror* for eight years and is now a freelance journalist covering health and medical issues for national newspapers and magazines. She lives with her husband and three children in South London. Simone can be contacted at www.yourbabyandchild.com.

potty
training
boys
the easy way

**Helping Your
Son Learn
Quickly—
Even If He's
a Late Starter**

LIFELONG BOOKS

Caroline Fertleman, MD & Simone Cave

Potty Training Boys the Easy Way
*Helping Your Son Learn Quickly—
Even If He's a Late Starter*

Caroline Fertleman, MD, and Simone Cave

Potty Training Boys the Easy Way is the only guide written
by a pediatrician for navigating the challenges unique to
potty training boys. You'll find an accessible, step-by-step
plan for getting your son trained quickly. Practical and
reassuring, Potty Training Boys the Easy Way is packed
with all the information a family needs to reach this
important milestone.

$11.95 • 144 pages • ISBN: 978-0-7382-1330-9

Available wherever books are sold

www.dacapopress.com